People in My Community/La gente de mi comunidad

Teacher/
El maestro

W9-ANU-969

JoAnn Early Macken
photographs by/fotografías de Gregg Andersen

Reading consultant/Consultora de lectura: Susan Nations, M.Ed., author/literacy coach/consultant

WEEKLY WR READER®
EARLY LEARNING LIBRARY

Please visit our web site at: www.garethstevens.com
For a free color catalog describing our list of high-quality books,
call 1-800-542-2595 (USA) or 1-800-387-3178 (Canada).

Library of Congress Cataloging-in-Publication Data

Macken, JoAnn Early, 1953-
    [Teacher. Spanish & English]
    Teacher = El maestro / by JoAnn Early Macken.
      p. cm. — (People in my community = La gente de mi comunidad)
    Summary: Photographs and simple text introduce the work of the teacher, who helps children learn
how to read, write, and count.
    Includes bibliographical references and index.
    ISBN-13: 978-0-8368-3675-2 (lib. bdg.)
    ISBN-10: 0-8368-3675-8 (lib. bdg.)
    ISBN-13: 978-0-8368-3689-9 (softcover)
    ISBN-10: 0-8368-3689-8 (softcover)
    1. Teachers—Juvenile literature. 2. Teaching—Vocational guidance—Juvenile literature. [1. Teachers.
2. Occupations. 3. Spanish language materials—Bilingual.] I. Title: Maestro. II. Title. III. People
in my community. Spanish & English.
    LB1775.M422218   2003
    371.1—dc21
                                                2002044911

Updated and reprinted in 2005.
First published in 2003 by
Weekly Reader® Books
An imprint of Gareth Stevens Publishing
1 Reader's Digest Road
Pleasantville, NY 10570-7000 USA

Copyright © 2003 by Weekly Reader® Early Learning Library

Art direction: Tammy West
Page layout: Katherine A. Goedheer
Photographer: Gregg Andersen
Editorial assistant: Diane Laska-Swanke
Translators: Colleen Coffey and Consuelo Carrillo

Printed in the United States of America

4 5 6 7 8 9 11 10 09 08 07

Note to Educators and Parents

Reading is such an exciting adventure for young children! They are beginning to integrate their oral language skills with written language. To encourage children along the path to early literacy, books must be colorful, engaging, and interesting; they should invite the young reader to explore both the print and the pictures.

People in My Community is a new series designed to help children read about the world around them. In each book young readers will learn interesting facts about some familiar community helpers.

Each book is specially designed to support the young reader in the reading process. The familiar topics are appealing to young children and invite them to read — and re-read — again and again. The full-color photographs and enhanced text further support the student during the reading process.

In addition to serving as wonderful picture books in schools, libraries, homes, and other places where children learn to love reading, these books are specifically intended to be read within an instructional guided reading group. This small group setting allows beginning readers to work with a fluent adult model as they make meaning from the text. After children develop fluency with the text and content, the book can be read independently. Children and adults alike will find these books supportive, engaging, and fun!

Una nota a los educadores y a los padres

¡La lectura es una emocionante aventura para los niños! En esta etapa están comenzando a integrar su manejo del lenguaje oral con el lenguaje escrito. Para fomentar la lectura desde una temprana edad, los libros deben ser vistosos, atractivos e interesantes; deben invitar al joven lector a explorar tanto el texto como las ilustraciones.

La gente de mi comunidad es una nueva serie pensada para ayudar a los niños a conocer el mundo que los rodea. En cada libro, los jóvenes lectores conocerán datos interesantes sobre el trabajo de distintas personas de la comunidad.

Cada libro ha sido especialmente diseñado para facilitar el proceso de lectura. La familiaridad con los temas tratados atrae la atención de los niños y los invita a leer — y releer — una y otra vez. Las fotografías a todo color y el tipo de letra facilitan aún más al estudiante el proceso de lectura.

Además de servir como fantásticos libros ilustrados en la escuela, la biblioteca, el hogar y otros lugares donde los niños aprenden a amar la lectura, estos libros han sido concebidos específicamente para ser leídos en grupos de instrucción guiada. Este contexto de grupos pequeños permite que los niños que se inician en la lectura trabajen con un adulto cuya fluidez les sirve de modelo para comprender el texto. Una vez que se han familiarizado con el texto y el contenido, los niños pueden leer los libros por su cuenta. ¡Tanto niños como adultos encontrarán que estos libros son útiles, entretenidos y divertidos!

— Susan Nations, M.Ed., author, literacy coach,
and consultant in literacy development

The teacher helps children learn in school. Children learn about reading, writing, and math.

- - - - - - - -

La maestra ayuda a los niños a aprender en la escuela. Los niños aprenden a leer y a escribir. También aprenden matemáticas.

Children all around the world go to school to learn from their teachers.

Los niños de todo el mundo van a la escuela para aprender de sus maestros.

The teacher reads books with the students. The teacher might use a **computer** to help students learn.

- - - - - - -

La maestra lee libros con los estudiantes. La maestra puede usar una **computadora** para ayudar a los niños a aprender.

**computer/
computadora**

Teachers answer questions.
Teachers also ask students
questions. If you know the
answer, raise your hand.

— — — — — — —

Los maestros contestan
preguntas. Ellos también
hacen preguntas a los
estudiantes. Si sabes la
respuesta, levanta la mano.

Some teachers teach many subjects, like math, reading, and writing. Some teachers teach just one subject, like art, science, or music.

▬ ▬ ▬ ▬ ▬ ▬ ▬

Algunos maestros enseñan muchas materias, tales como matemáticas, lectura y escritura. Otros enseñan sólo una materia como arte, ciencia o música.

Sometimes a teacher takes children on a field trip. They might visit a zoo or a museum. Field trips help children learn more about their subjects.

- - - - - - - -

Algunas veces la maestra lleva a los niños de excursión. Ellos pueden visitar un zoológico o un museo. Ir de excursión ayuda a los niños a aprender más sobre las materias.

Teachers work at school and at home. At home, they correct papers and tests. They plan what to teach.

— — — — — — —

Los maestros trabajan en la escuela y en la casa. En casa, corrigen la tarea y los exámenes. Ellos planifican sus clases.

Teachers meet with adults
to tell them how much their
children are learning.

– – – – – – – –

Los maestros se reunen con
los adultos para explicarles
lo que sus hijos han aprendido.

It's fun to share what you know.

— — — — — — —

Es divertido compartir lo que tú sabes.

Glossary/Glosario

field trip — a visit made by a teacher and students to learn by seeing something

excursión — visita que hacen el maestro y sus estudiantes a un lugar para aprender más sobre algún tema

museum — a place to see objects of interest and value

museo — lugar donde se pueden ver objetos interesantes y valiosos

subjects — areas of learning, such as art, math, or science

materias — temas de estudio, tales como arte, matemáticas, o ciencias

For More Information/Más información

Fiction Books/Libros de ficción

Henkes, Kevin. *Lilly's Purple Plastic Purse.*
  New York: Greenwillow Books, 1996.

Nonfiction Books/Libros de no ficción

Deedrick, Tami. *Teachers.*
  Mankato, Minn.: Bridgestone Books, 1998.
Hayward, Linda. *A Day in the Life of a Teacher.*
  New York: Dorling Kindersley, 2001.
Liebman, Daniel. *I Want to Be a Teacher.*
  Willowdale, Ont.: Firefly Books, 2001.
Maynard, Christopher. *Jobs People Do.*
  New York: DK Publishing, 2001.

Web Sites/Páginas Web

Bureau of Labor Statistics Career Information
http://stats.bls.gov/k12/html/red_002.htm
What teachers do, how they prepare for the job, more
information about teaching

Index/Índice

About the Author/Información sobre la autora

JoAnn Early Macken is the author of children's poetry, two rhyming picture books, *Cats on Judy* and *Sing-Along Song* and various other nonfiction series. She teaches children to write poetry and received the Barbara Juster Esbensen 2000 Poetry Teaching Award. JoAnn is a graduate of the MFA in Writing for Children Program at Vermont College. She lives in Wisconsin with her husband and their two sons.

JoAnn Early Macken es autora de poesía para niños. Ha escrito dos libros de rimas con ilustraciones, *Cats on Judy* y *Sing-Along Song* y otras series de libros educativos para niños. Ella enseña a los niños a escribir poesía y ha ganado el Premio Barbara Juster Esbensen en el año 2000. JoAnn se graduó con el título de "MFA" en el programa de escritura infantil de Vermont College. Vive en Wisconsin con su esposo y sus dos hijos.